AF488454

Forward

"Our vision is to source and carry delicious wines that are not found on grocery and chain store shelves and that represent a good value for their quality levels. This business will also be centered on providing superior service levels above all other retailers by ensuring customers have wine savvy staff that can provide guidance and services for food pairings, gifts, private parties. " (excerpt from original business plan, 2010).

We opened for business on July 5, 2011 after spending most of 2009-10 planning, crunching numbers, taking classes at the Culinary Institute in Napa Valley and visiting similar businesses both in the Dallas area and Napa and Sonoma. In the end the business plan was thrown out of the window (we will say, however, that the time spent was magical).

The major issue was timing. We bought an existing business only for its location and closed this operating bakery. We really wanted this site, as it was the perfect location for our concept. However, we were in the early stages of trying to obtain a winery permit, and it would take until November to be acquired. So, we spent the first four months learning many of the whats and hows serving lunch and desserts. A fine wine lifestyle shop we were not. If we were to survive we needed to sell something! We became a restaurant by default and opened for dinner on November 18. Oh, yes, now the fun starts!

Almost 9 years later, on March 16, 2020 we informed our family and friends that we could not continue the business with the loss of traffic from the Covid pandemic.

We loved our time as restaurateurs and wine enthusiasts. This recipe book was inspired originally by a request from Katelynn French of Midland, our granddaughter. However the final product became a life story ready to be told, and we hope you enjoy the story as much as the fantastic recipes.

Days of wine & roses

Sip & Savor

Recipes and sidebars from a wine
country inspired dinner house

John Weeks

Sip & Savor

Appetizers Soups & Salads

Our first efforts in this business focused on apps, small plates and salads. As we gained experience many of the recipes were abandoned. This section captures the best we offered over the years.

Tomato Soup

Flatbreads

Wow, did I spend a lot of time on flatbreads! Initially I was looking for a unique recipe that would be a quick bake and not require any special equipment. I ran across this Argentinian style "Fugazza" and ran with it.

We had 2 large deck ovens to support us and we kept one at 450F at all times. Our turn time goal for orders was anywhere from 8 to 18 minutes. Flatbreads needed to get out in 10 minutes. This recipe allowed us to make the dough and store it in the reefer until we were ready to bake. We also could par bake the bread and finish in the oven in 4 to 5 minutes, turning out a crispy exterior and soft middle that held up very well with any toppings.

Ingredients (Doubled recipe, can be halved)
2 C water 105°F
2 tsp sugar
4 tsp yeast
5 1/3 C bread flour
10 tbs olive oil
4 tsp salt

1.   Add sugar to warm water. Add yeast to sugar water and stir....let sit for 10 minutes until bubbly.
2.   Place flour in stand mixer bowl. Add oil and stir just until incorporated. Sprinkle salt over flour mixture.
3.   Add yeast mixture to dough and knead with dough hook until it comes together. Stir and mix to incorporate.
4.   Turn out on a lightly floured surface and knead for 5 minutes until springy. Place in oiled bowl, cover with plastic wrap and put in warm place for at least 30 minutes or until doubled in size.
5.   Turn out and separate into 4 servings. Plastic wrap and store in reefer.
6.   When ready to bake, spread out on a dry parchment paper into a rectangle or circle.
7.   Make dimples in bread with your fingers. Be sure the dough has no breaks or holes.
8.   Bake at 450 for 5 minutes. At this point they can be cooled, wrapped and stored in the reefer, OR, they can be topped and finished as per each recipe, typically baked for another 4 to 5 minutes.

Now that we have the flatbread, we need to create the toppings.

Spread - The glue to it all. Let's go with great spreads and flavors....spicy white bean hummus, fruit preserves, pestos, cheese spreads, cream cheese mixes

Focal points - The star attractions including salmon, crab, shrimp, pulled pork, beef short rib, etc. We should always have a spring seasonal garden offer too.

Garnish - Always remember sweet, salty, sour, bitter and savory.

Sweet: preserves, fruits, candied nuts, honey,

Salty: salty nuts, cured meats and fish (like bacon, prosciutto, & sardine), parmesan, olive, finishing salt

Sour: pickled veggies, vinegars, citrus fruits, wine, Bitter: greens and herbs, garlic,

Savory: meats, cheeses, mushrooms, beans, olives, nuts, roasted veggies, reductions

Some of the more popular ones over the years.....

Caprese: tomato, quarters, grated mozzarella, finished with basil leaves, EVOO, flake salt

Fig & Goat Cheese: Fig preserve, goat cheese, torn prosciutto, finished with rosemary, arugula, scallion

Steak: Tenderloin tips, horseradish cream cheese, mushroom slices, caramelized onion, finished with chives, flake salt

1. Shelf Life   par cooked - 3 days   frozen - 1 month

Blue Cheese Tart

This is our first amuse bouche (small bite). We served this free for several months after we opened. It's still one of the easiest and tastiest bites we created.

Brown Butter Tart crust
6 tbsp. unsalted butter, cubed
3 tbsp. water
1 tbsp. canola oil
1 tbsp. sugar
⅛ tsp. kosher salt
1 cup flour

Filling:
1 C cream
1 oz blue cheese
1oz brie
1 egg and 1 egg yolk
pine nuts, basil, chiffonade and S&P to taste

Make the crust: Heat oven to 400°. Stir butter, water, oil, sugar, and salt in a heatproof bowl; bake until butter is bubbling and lightly brown at edges, about 20 minutes. Remove from oven and stir in flour until dough comes together. Press dough into bottom and up sides of five 4″ tart pans (or one large 9″ tart). Using a fork, prick dough all over. Bake until cooked through, 10–12 minutes; let cool.
Build the tarts: Whisk cream, blue cheese, brie and eggs together. Pour into the tart shells to fill. Sprinkle pine nuts and basil on top and lightly salt and pepper. Bake at 350 for 10 minutes or until filling has solidified. Serve warm.

Tarts can be made ahead and warmed at 350 for 5 to 7 minutes to serve.
Filling can be made ahead and refrigerated one day.

Dips

Spinach & Beet dip

Makes 4 cups for 10 to 12
2 cup thawed, chopped frozen spinach
3 cups cooked beets, cubed small
12 ounces cream cheese
1/2 cup sour cream and 1/2 cup mayonnaise
2/3 cup grated Parmesan
1 teaspoon red pepper flakes and 1/2 teaspoon salt
1/2 teaspoon garlic powder
   Note: To cook bets, select medium to large beets and trim the greens off. Wrap in foil and cook in 400F oven for 45 to 60 minutes, checking for tenderness with a toothpick. Cool to touch and then wipe peel off with a paper towel or kitchen cloth.
   November 19, 2011

Spicy White Bean Hummus

There once existed a wine bar on Highway 29 in St. Helena named AKA Bistro. Teresa and I would drop in to get a glass of wine and this app, which I recreated for Sip & Savor.
   1/4 cup chopped scallion whites
   4 tablespoons fresh lemon juice
   2 tablespoons tahini
   1/2 teaspoon dried oregano
   1/4 teaspoon ground cumin
   1/8 teaspoon salt and black pepper
   Red pepper flakes to taste
   4 cups Great Northern white beans, rinsed and drained
   1 garlic clove peeled

   In a blender or food processor, puree all together and taste for salt and lemon juice balance.
   November 19, 2011
   Revised May 2016

Steamed Artichoke

It was at the La Playa Inn in Carmel, California over Labor Day weekend, 1994 that Teresa first tasted steamed artichokes. La Playa also served as the place that I proposed to her, and our honeymoon destination. So, was it me or the artichoke that she said "Yes" to?

4-6 artichokes, trimmed (see below) , serving whole artichoke per person
Artichoke stems, trimmed
2 lemons, cut in half
1 TBS salt
  Recipe
To trim an artichoke
  Using a bread knife, cut the stem off so that artichoke sits square on a flat surface.
  then cut the top 1" off the leaves. Using scissors, cut the barbs off the outer leaves,
  about 2 rows in.

To prepare:

1. Put artichokes (plate to hold down) in simmerring water (add lemons and juice and salt to water). Artichokes should sit in 2 inches of water. Use a plate to hold under water if necessary. Simmer for 25 minutes.
2. Turn over and simmer another 25 minutes until paring knife glides through stem easily. Remove and drain.
3. When cool remove inner leaves and choke to make a bowl by using a teaspoon to cut them out.
4. To store, cut a lemon slice and place inside cleaned bowl to keep it from discoloring.

April 2016

Date Stuffed Mushrooms

I left this recipe as written for the restaurant to show how we prepped for service to get food out quicker.

Date Stuffed Mushrooms

20 Medium cap mushrooms, stem removed and mushroom dry cleaned

1/2 C chopped dates

2 Tbs mayonnaise

1 shallot, minced

1/2 C parmesan cheese, grated

1/2 C bacon, cooked and crumbled

1 C panko crumbs

EVOO

Black pepper

Parmesan cheese, fine zest

Combine dates, mayo, shallot, grated parmesan cheese, and bacon and hold refrigerated.

On order:

Fill 4 caps with stuffing, cover with panko crums and drizzle with EVOO and bake at 400/425 for 6-8 minutes

Plate and zest parmesan over caps. Add black pepper and serve

June 2019

Tomato Soup in Puff Pastry

Serves 6 to 8

½ cup butter unsalted

½ lb. Yellow onions-sliced

6 ea. Garlic cloves

1 bay leaf

½ Tbl. Whole black peppercorns or 2 tsp. ground pepper or to taste

1 tsp. Dried thyme leaves

1/4 cup tomato paste

2 ½ ib. tomatoes-ripe, cored, and quartered or 2-28oz cans high quality such as San Marzano.

4 cups heavy cream

2- 4 Tbl. Butter or to taste

4 tsp salt or to taste

2 tsp. Ground white pepper or skip but this adds quite a bit of flavor

1 lb. Puff pastry-or store bought sheets

1 Egg- beaten with 1 Tbl. of water

Procedures:

Melt ½ C butter in a large stockpot over medium-low heat. Add the onions, garlic, thyme, bay leaf and peppercorns; cover and cook for about 5 minutes. Do not let the onions color.

Add tomato paste and lightly "toast" the tomato paste to cook out the raw flavor then add tomatoes. Simmer over low heat for 30 minutes, until the tomatoes and onions are very soft and broken down.

Puree in a blender or food processor, then strain. Return the soup to the pot.

Add the cream, salt, white pepper and remaining butter to taste. Bring soup to a simmer then remove from heat.

From here down is the kitchen handling, cooking and presentation aspects of this dish. They are not part of the soup recipe in and of itself....you can just reheat the soup and go!! However, the puff pastry presentation is what made this dish so exceptional and I wouldn't leave it out, especially if you are entertaining.

Allow the soup to cool for two hours or overnight in the refrigerator.

Preheat oven to 425 degrees.

Divide the soup among six 8-ounce soup cups or bowls.

Roll out the puff pastry to 1/4 inch. Cut into 6 rounds slightly larger than your cups.

Paint around the edge of the dough with the egg wash and turn the circles, egg wash side down, over the tops of the cups, pulling lightly on the sides to make the dough somewhat tight like a drum. Try not to allow the dough to touch the soup.

Bake for 15 minutes, until the dough is golden brown. Do not open the oven in the first several minutes of cooking as the dough may fall. Serve immediately.

Soup quality shelf life refrigerated 5 days

November 2012, revised Sept 2016, redoux for home use October 2021 and revised for home use August 2022

Katelynn's Wedge Salad

This became somewhat iconic for us over the years and was a best seller. I affectionately call this "Katelynn's Salad" for my first granddaughter as she always ordered it when she dined with us.

WEDGE SALAD

1/4 cut wedge of iceberg lettuce, chilled
Creamy dressing to cover (see Recipe)
1 Apple wood smoked bacon, crumbled
6 Candied pecans
1oz Blue cheese crumbles
2oz Seasonal fruit
Balsamic drizzle

Build
Place wedge center plate, inside up
Drizzle dressing over wedge to partially cover, acting as "glue"
Spread bacon crumbles, pecans and blue cheese crumbles over wedge
Place seasonal fruit around wedge
Drizzle reduced balsamic vinegar across entire salad and serve

Cream of Jalapeno Soup

8 Servings
Ingredients
4 jalapeno peppers, skinned and seeded
1 red pepper, skinned and seeded
1/2 small onion, rough chop
2 clove garlic, rough chop
6 C stock (Vegetable preferred, or chicken)
1 Tbs house seasoning and 1 tsp cumin

Finish
1/2 C heavy cream, 2-3 Tbs blue cheese and a squeeze lime
S&P

Garnish
1 TBS Tomato, diced
1 Tsp red pepper, diced
1 TBS Cilantro, minced
Cook peppers and remove meat. Discard skins.
Saute peppers and onion medium low 5 minutes
Add garlic and saute 1 minute
Add stock, house seasoning and cumin and simmer 5 minutes
Salt to taste
Allow to cool some and blend smooth and hold.
Plating

Combine 1 cup soup, cream and blue cheese and heat through
Plate and squeeze lime over soup, garnish and serve.

September 2018
Revised Oct 2021 to serve 8
Updated Oct 2024

Garden Ranch Dressing

We grew many of our own herbs and used them to bring that freshness in our recipes. If you have any space at all that gets a few hours of sunlight you can grow many of them. We had oregano, sage, rosemary, thyme, and occasionally arugula, strawberries and tomatoes.

2 c mayonnaise

2 c sour cream

1 c buttermilk

2 Tbsp RW Vinegar

2 clove garlic

1/2 c parsley, minced

1/2 c cilantro, minced

1/4 c oregano, minced

1/4 c thyme, minced

1 small tomato, quartered

2 slices onion, cubed

Pinch of S&P

1 Tbs House Seasoning

1. In a medium bowl, stir together mayonnaise, sour cream and buttermilk Add vinegar until smooth.
2. Combine the herbs and spices. Mix into dressing.
3. Chop the tomato, and onion in a food processor until finely minced and mix into dressing.
4. Chill for at least an hour before serving.

June 2019

Sip Salad Dressing

This is a very basic salad dressing that can be modified easily. It is lighter than most as the ratio of sour cream to mayonnaise is very high. The use of buttermilk gives it a nice tang and the tiny bit of sugar helps to balance it with the Sip wedge salad ingredients.

Ingredients
4 TBS mayo
1 C sour cream
2 C buttermilk
2 tsp Dijon mustard
4 clove garlic, minced
1 tsp sugar
S&P to taste (generally 1/2 tsp each)

Recipe
Mix together and store for use

Shelf life 2 weeks refrigerated

Summer Harvest Salad

Ingredients:

1 Block of watermelon 1" X 1" X 3"
Ginger syrup
3 Cherry tomatoes
3 Mozzarella balls
3 Melon balls
Mint leaves, whole
Sea Salt

 Make ginger syrup with 1 C sugar, 2 C water and 2 Tbs minced ginger. Steep and strain and hold for service.
Cut cherry tomatoes in half
Make melon balls

 At Service:
 Place watermelon block center plate
Place mozzarella ball, tomato half and melon ball on watermelon
Place remaining mozzarella, tomato and melon around watermelon
Drizzle with ginger syrup
Place mint leaf as garnish
Sprinkle with finishing salt and serve

June 2018

Wine Program

"This business will be centered on two key differences; one, to source and sell uniquely delicious wines at great prices that are not commonly found in the market area and, two, by engaging our customers through lunches, regular weekly tastings, food and wine pairings, catered and wine-maker events, and charity fundraisers."

This was our original business plan, and we did indeed accomplish all of this. The final step was our wine club, which offered dinners, private tastings and pairings. Teresa and I spent many weeks and months in Napa, scouring wineries for great wines, obtaining certifications from the Culinary Institute of America at Greystone, and becoming comfortable in the lifestyle of Napa Valley.

Entrees and Sides

At our core we were a wine bistro, and as we built the fine wine program we refined our entrees. We sold the basics like filet mignon, rib eye steaks, fresh Alaskan salmon and Pacific halibut and shellfish from the east coast. But I am most proud of our composed dishes created from scratch, such as our short ribs, crab cakes and gnocchi. I've added many of our sauce and condiment recipes here too.

Cooking Steaks

Cooking Steak at Sip & Savor

Our number one menu item for years was our top choice Beef Tenderloin (Filet Mignon). I couldn't leave out a mention for our cooking process for tenderloins and ribeyes as you will not see a recipe for these in this collection. You can find thousands of lessons for cooking beef and I am sure they are great for their authors. However our focus at Sip was more singular.

We needed to cook beef to the perfect temperature every time as a "refire" would literally shut down our 2 person kitchen and we just couldn't afford for that to happen. So I devised a method using sous vide cooking to, essentially, prep steaks in advance of knowing what was going to be ordered. This meant that we would clean, cut and sous vide steaks to a rare temp and hold them in the reefer until they were ordered. Once ordered, we could then take them from refrigerated to done in as little as 6 minutes for rare to around 12 minutes for well done.

All of our steaks were seasoned with our house seasoning, hit the saute pan with an oil and butter mixture to get seared, and then finished in the 450F oven. Our great head cook Leo was so good at this that we probably achieved 99% perfection. Steaks that did come back were sometimes the wrong temp, but most times they were right on.

Crab Cakes

We bought our crab from The Crab Broker out of Las Vegas, typically paying $27 per pound for Alaskan Red King Crab legs. Very pricey, but I found that through trial and error there was no crab that could compete with the taste and texture of Red King Crab. I recommend using Red King crabmeat or other west coast crabmeat but, any lump crab will work.

2C crab meat, lump or leg
1 Egg, blended
 2 Tbs parsley, minced
1/4C red onion, minced
3/4 C Ritz crackers, crumbled

Instructions:
 Combine all ingredients GENTLY to keep lumps together

Prep:
Cakes are to be 3 ounces
425 oven, cook first side 5 minutes, 2nd side 3 minutes

September 2019
Modified quantities for home use 4/2020

Scallops & Fettuccine

We bought our scallops straight off the boats in Maine and New Hampshire, delivered in 40 pound burlap bags. These were U8's or U10's depending on availability. This means 8 or 10 to a pound, and we served 5 to 6 ounces per dish. We also made our own pasta which would only take 3 to 4 minutes of boil to be ready, unlike dry pasta at 8 to 12 minutes.

Ingredients:
2 1/2 ounces fettucine, fresh made
1/2 C fresh lemon zest
2 Tsp capers
1 TBS EVOO
S&P
Fresh herb like parsley, thyme, sage
Three 1 to 1 1/2 ounce U10 scallops

Instructions:

1. Sear scallops in butter/ oil blend for 2 minutes on one side, then flip and sear for another 2 minutes. You are looking for a translucent middle (medium rare). If you overcook them you can use them as golf balls.
2. Remove from saute pan when finished but keep oils in pan for finish work.
3. Cook fettucine in pasta water until al dente, about 3 minutes (longer for dry pasta)
4. Place fettucine in saute pan, add EVOO, lemon zest, capers and pasta water if needed and toss.

Plating:

Place fettucine in bowl
Place scallops at 2pm, 6pm and 10pm.
Finishing salt and serve.

September 2018

Shrimp and Grits

Ingredients:
    4 shrimp, peeled and deveined
1 1/2 C finished creamy polenta (see recipe)
2 TBS Bacon Jam (see recipe)
4 Cherry tomatoes, halved
    Finishing salt

Instructions:

1. Heat par cooked polenta
2. Saute shrimp in garlic butter until just cooked. Shrimp should be moist and just cooked. Requires watching closely. Just before shrimp are finished add tomato halves to cook through, about 30 seconds.
3. Heat bacon jam.
4. Plate polenta in bowl, add shrimp tails up in center.
5. Place bacon jam in center of shrimp.
6. Add tomatoes on top, allowing to spill over.
7. Add finishing salt and serve

September 2018

Cheddar Cheese Polenta

9 cups water
2 1/2 cups polenta (stone ground cornmeal)
10 tablespoons butter
1 1/2 C milk, room temp
1 1/2 cup sharp white cheddar cheese, shredded
1 Tbs Kosher salt
1 Tsp white pepper

Instructions:
 Bring water to boil and add salt
Whisk in polenta slowly to reduce lumping
Reduce heat to slight simmer, and stir often, for about 20 minutes
Remove pot from heat when polenta is al dente
Add cheese, milk and butter. Whisk until incorporated
Add salt and white pepper to taste.
Reserve for service in refrigerator

At Service:

1. Measure out 1 cup and put in sauce pan to heat

2. Add just enough veggie stock to loosen

3. Heat and serve

Refrigerated shelf - 1 week

Sept 2016

Mac & Cheese Sauce

I am not including a recipe for pasta since it requires special equipment such as rollers, cutters and extruders. We did make all of our own pasta and you can absolutely tell the difference. If you have the inclination you should go down this path. Fresh pasta also gets out of the kitchen fast...from 3 to 5 minutes and its ready to go. If you use dry pasta (store bought) follow the directions on the box to get al dente results.

Ingredients

1# pasta
16oz Evaporated Milk
2 eggs
1 tsp dry mustard

1# ES cheddar, grated
1/2# gruyere, grated
1/2# parmesan, grated
1 Tbs cornstarch
8 Tbs butter

Instructions

Cook pasta in lowest water level possible, to al dente. Most of the water will be absorbed. Do not rinse out pan after cooked.

Blend milk, eggs and dry mustard. Add to pasta.

Toss 1/2 of grated cheeses with cornstarch, add to pasta in batches until melted.

Add butter to pasta and melt. Serve hot

Beef Short Ribs

We loved making these long bone short ribs. We would prep the marinade and put the ribs in for 12 hours, and then cook them off the next day. We reduced the marinade down to concentrate the flavor and added it to our mushroom gravy. Really a great dish but pretty labor intensive. Served over risotto.

Ingredients for 8 servings:

3 Tbs Cooking oil for the onion saute
S&P
8 short ribs
1 bottle wine
6 C stock
2 onions, rough cut
4 garlic cloves, chopped
2 C tomato, rough chop
Rosemary sprig

Marinate:
Salt & pepper short ribs and sear in oil. Set aside.
Saute onion until tender.
Add garlic and saute 1 minute.
Add tomatoes & vegetable or beef stock and whisk to combine off heat.
Add short ribs and cover with liquids.
Add rosemary and marinate in reefer 12 hours.

Instructions"

1. Remove ribs and heat braising liquids to simmer.
2. Add back short ribs, cover with aluminum foil.
3. Braise for 2 1/2 hours at 325F.
4. Strain and defat braising liquid and hold for mushroom gravy.

Sep 2017

Spinach Gnocchi

I left this recipe in restaurant volumes as it is labor intensive and probably not worth your time in small quantities. Once made, these can be frozen and held for months. This yields about 80 gnocchi

8 ounces spinach with stems on and 1 C spinach water

1 tsp. salt	¼ tsp. freshly grated nutmeg
2 Tbs unsalted butter	1 1/2 cup flour
3 large eggs	1/2 C grated Parmigiano-Reggiano

Instructions:

1. Cook spinach in pot of lightly salted boiling water for 3 minutes.
2. Drain spinach and put in blender. Blend and strain. Reserve strained liquid and puree separately. You should have 1/2 C puree and 1/2 C spinach water. Add 1/2 C water to make a full cup of spinach water.
3. In pot, combine the spinach water, salt, nutmeg and butter and bring to a boil over high heat. Add flour all at once and beat the dough with a wooden spoon until it is thick and comes away from the side of the pan.
4. Cook, stirring to dry out the dough, about 30 seconds. Let cool slightly, about 5 minutes.
5. With a stand mixer with the paddle attachment, beat 1 egg into the dough on medium low until incorporated. Beat in cup of the cheese and another egg until blended, beat in puree, then beat in the last egg until the dough is very smooth.
6. Bring a large pot of salted water to a boil. Transfer the dough to a pastry bag with the large round tip. Let rest in fridge for 5 minutes to firm up.
7. Reduce the heat to maintain a gentle simmer. Carefully hold the bag over the water and press out the dough, using a small sharp knife to cut it into 1½-inch lengths before it drops into the pot.
8. Simmer the gnocchi for 1 minute after they float. Transfer the gnocchi to paper towels and let dry and cool. Lay on parchment paper lined sheet pan and cover with parchment. Freeze and transfer to freezer bag for later use.

John's customized recipe
December 29, 2016

Loaded Potato Gnocchi

Ingredients
2 large russet potatoes   Pinch of sea salt
1/2 C flour   2 large egg yolks (approximately 1 oz)

Bake potatoes at 400F for 60 minutes. Cool slightly and scoop out hot potato and, using a ricer or masher, process potato into a fine mixture into a large bowl or smooth surface.
Add flour and egg and bring together as you would pasta. Season with salt. Do not knead dough as overworked potato will become gummy.
Once the dough comes together, roll it out with your hands as you would cookie dough, to a diameter around 1 1/2 inches. Cut your gnocchi with a knife or bench scraper.

Instructions:

1. In simmering salted water, drop gnocchi in and cook for about 1 minute until they float to the top. Once risen, use an ice bath to stop the cooking process. Use a parchment lined sheet pan to set gnocchi on and then freeze, or use within 2 days. Keep refrigerated if not freezing.
2. When you are ready to serve, Place 6 to 8 gnocchi in a oiled and buttered saute pan and cook until browned on all sides, about 5 minutes.

Finishing Ingredients:

Smoked bacon, cooked crisp and crumbled
Scallion greens, sliced on bias
Creme fraiche dollop
     Place on plate and add toppings of crumbled bacon, sliced scallion and creme fraiche or sour cream. Lightly salt and serve.

Thrice Cooked Sweet Potato Casserole

Ingredients:
5# potatoes, peeled and cut into 8ths

Sauce:
2 C brown sugar
3 sticks (3/4#) butter
1 Tbs House Seasoning
1/2 C water or OJ
1/3 C Bourbon

Bouquet garni:
1 tsp nutmeg
1 tsp Chinese 5 spice
2 1/2 tsp cinnamon
1 tsp orange peel
1/tsp lemon peel

Instructions:

1. In a pot of simmering water, cook potatoes for 5 minutes until semi soft. Do not cook through.
2. Combine bouqet garni items in cheesecloth and tie to hold together with kitchen twine.
3. Separately, simmer other ingredients and Bouquet Garni together to make sauce.
4. Remove garni. Layer potatoes and sauce. Add pats of butter & additional brown sugar as desired.
5. Bake at 350F for 45 minutes. Cool, cover and refrigerate or take to room temperature if immediately baking again.
6. When ready to serve, take to room temp, add pats of butter and brown sugar or marshmallow topping and bake at 375 until heated through.

Original 2016
Revised 2020 for 16 peeps

Brussel Sprouts

These are so awesome to cook! You can blanch, roast, steam, bake, grill and braise these guys. And you can flavor them in many ways. We liked to "candy" them to deliver a balancing sweetness to their bitterness.

Approximate Ratios per serving (I recommend tripling this to serve 4):

2 Tbs Sugar
1 Tbs Butter
10 Brussels
3 Tbs Candied bacon
3 Tbs Shallots, sliced thin
1 Tbs Garlic, minced
Squeeze of lemon
Parmesan cheese, finely grated
Pinch of sea salt
   Instructions:

1. Trim and cut brussels in half. Blanch in boiling salted water for 5 minutes. Drain and rinse.
2. Melt butter and sugar, add brussels and saute for 1 minute on medium high.
3. Add candied bacon, shallots and garlic and place in 425F oven to finish cooking, about 3 minutes. Test for doneness.
4. Plate, and add a squeeze of lemon, parmesan and pinch of salt.

Modified for home use April 2024

Sauces and Condiments

Flavor, Flavor, Flavor. Every dish is all about judicious use of spices, herbs and sauces. We incorporated house made sauces, aiolis and gravies in almost every dish. We also created many finishing touches with fruit reductions, reduced balsamic vinegar and herb oils. It is these inoculations of flavor that make most dishes. The only times we moved away from flavor punches is when the main dish, usually from the sea, needed to stand alone for its delicacy and texture. There is a reason why there are thousands of sauces, condiments and mixes available on the grocery shelves.

Bacon Jam

Ingredients:

2# bacon
1 C each shallot and sweet onion, minced
2 garlic clove, minced
1/4 C currants
1/2 bottle red wine, low tannins such as sangiovese, pinot noir or merlot
1/4 C bourbon (or apple cider vinegar for a non alcoholic jam)
1/4 C each maple syrup and molasses(optional)
1/2 C brown sugar
1/8 C (2 oz) red wine vinegar
2 tsp smoked paprika and ground black pepper
1 tbs fresh thyme (or 2 Tsp dried)

Instructions:

1. Cut bacon into 1/4" strips. Cook bacon slowly until rendered (soapy). Set aside.
2. Retain 1/4 C bacon fat for shallot / onion mix.
3. Add shallot and onion to pan, cook over medium heat until caramelized.
4. Add the garlic and cook one more minute.. Add brown sugar and smoked paprika and stir.
5. Off heat, add maple syrup, molasses and bourbon and stir. Add wine, currants and bacon and simmer until it comes together. App 1 hour.
6. Add RW vinegar, pepper and thyme and stir. Cool.
7. Remove to food processor and pulse until mixture is jam consistency. Jar and store refrigerated for up to 1 month.

September 2017 ver6
October 2024 redoux for home use

Mushroom Gravy

We made this for our Beef Short Ribs, but we also used it in other menu items.

Ingredients:

4 Tbs olive oil
2 medium onion, finely minced (1 cup)
2 pinch rubbed dried sage
2 pinch dried thyme
2 Tbs minced or crushed garlic
20 medium-large mushrooms, wiped clean and minced (a generous 1/2 pound)
2 pinch salt
4 Tbs cornstarch
2 quarts vegetable stock (or chicken stock)

Instructions
1) Place a medium saucepan over medium heat for about a minute, then add the oil and swirl to coat the pan. Toss in the onion and dried herbs, and sauté for 5 minutes, or until the onion softens.

2) Stir in the garlic, and cook, stirring often, for another minute or so, until the garlic disappears into the mix visually and gives off an aroma.

3) Add the mushrooms and salt, stir to distribute, and cover the pot. Cook for 10 minutes over medium heat, stirring once in a while, until the mushrooms cook down into the onion, and they give off a visible amount of juices.

4) Meanwhile, place the cornstarch in a small bowl, and slowly pour in about a cup of the stock, stirring constantly with a small whisk until the mixture is completely smooth.

5) Pour the stock into the mushroom mixture and let it come to a boil uncovered over medium heat. When it boils, turn the heat to medium-low, and drizzle in the cornstarch slurry, stirring constantly with a wooden spoon.

Horseradish Cream Sauce

Here is my restaurant version for a horseradish condiment. I've more recently moved to using prepared horseradish from a jar as it is more readily available. But if you want the real thing, use this.

To process the root:

One horseradish root, about 3 ounces, peeled and grated through a fine mesh.
1/4C white vinegar, used to preserve the horseradish.
1 Tsp sea salt
Combine the above ingredients

To make the cream sauce:

One recipe of the processed root, or prepared horseradish to taste, about 1/2 cup.
2C sour cream
Juice from 2 lemons

Combine and whisk and hold refrigerated for up to 2 weeks.

Aug 2019, updated 2024

Remoulade Sauce & Red Pepper Aioli

Remoulade Sauce, spicy

2 C mayonnaise
1/4 C Dijon mustard
2 Tbs lemon juice
2 Tbs hot sauce such as Franks
2 Tbs Sip mustard (see Whole Grain Dijon Mustard)
3 cloves garlic, minced
1 Tbs capers, minced
1 Tbs worcestershire sauce
2 Tsp smoked paprika
2 Tsp salt

Whisk everything together and hold refrigerated for service

September 2019

Red Pepper Aioli (for steamed artichokes, etc)

1 red pepper or 6 small sweet mini peppers, broiled and skins removed
1 C mayo
1/4 C onion diced or 1 Tbs onion powder
2 garlic cloves minced or 2 Tsp garlic powder
2 Tbs lemon juice

Put in blender and puree. Chill and serve.

Updated Feb 2024

Blueberry Port Steak Sauce

Ingredients:
2 Tbs Grape seed oil or other neutral oil
2 cloves garlic, minced
2 tsp. chili flakes

3 cups beef broth
3/4 cup port wine
1 cup balsamic vinegar

4 1/2 cups blueberries
1/4 C brown sugar
1/2 tsp. cinnamon
1 sprig fresh rosemary

Instructions:

1. In a large saucepan saute minced garlic and chili flakes lightly in oil over medium heat. Add beef broth, balsamic vinegar and port wine
2. Turn the heat to high and cook until the liquid is reduced by about half. Add blueberries, cinnamon, rosemary and sugar and cook approximately 20 minutes until the blueberries break apart and the sauce thickens.
3. Work sauce through a fine mesh sieve to get most of the pulp out to thicken the sauce. If necessary cook sauce down for another 15 minutes to thicken.

1 day room temp
7 days refrigerated

May 2019

Whole Grain Dijon Mustard

This is awesome on a charcuterie board, or on most meat proteins

Ingredients:

1/2 c mustard seed
1/2 c white wine
1/2 c mild vinegar (champagne, white wine, white)
1/4 c dry mustard
1 tsp black garlic salt
2 tsp brown sugar

1. Place mustard seed, wine and vinegar in container and soak seeds overnight.
2. Place seed mixture and all other ingredients in food processor or blender and puree to a chunky consistency (seeds should still have form)
3. Place in jar and refrigerate for 5 days.
4. Can store for months

June 2017

Celebrations

Some of the best times at Sip & Savor were wedding proposals, engagements, bridal and baby showers, birthdays, retirements, and celebrations of health. We were privileged to be a part of so many celebrations of life.

Teresa and I often recall the couple that used Sip & Savor over the years to propose marriage, celebrate their wedding day, and stop by for a bottle of champagne on their way home from the hospital with their newborn baby.

We also will never forget our son Justin proposing to his now wife Krista, and we are so fortunate to now live a short 5 minute golf cart drive away from them and two of our grandchildren, Beckett and Leighton.

And so many planning meetings to be sure everything went perfectly from recipes to quantities, timing and special requests. You want to do a murder mystery? Sure. We are opening your 1976 Cabernet in celebration of your defeat of cancer? Is it still good? You know it is supposed to rain on your outdoor wedding, right Randy?

Desserts

Desserts are a tough category as they usually require baking, pastry doughs and shells, and many complex recipes. We had just a few desserts that withstood the test of time, and we stuck with them for years, making only slight variations depending upon the season. Here we have three of our best desserts.

Cheesecake

Graham cracker crust

1 3/4 C graham crackers, crumbed

3 Tbs butter, melted

1/2 Tsp salt

Using a springform pan, place parchment on bottom and grease.

Combine all above ingredients and press into pan and refrigerate.

Cheesecake filling

2# (four 8 oz packages) cream cheese

1 C (8oz) goat cheese

1 Tbs lemon juice

1 Tbs vanilla

2 C (14oz) sugar

6 eggs, cold

3/4 C (6 oz) heavy cream

In mixer, combine cheeses, lemon juice & vanilla. Mix on low until roughly combined.

Increase speed to medium and blend for 5 minutes. Scrape bowl midway.

Reduce speed to medium low and add sugar to combine.

Add whisked eggs slowly until combined on low speed, about 3 minutes.

Heat cream to a boil and add to low speed mixer. Chill.

Bake

Oven at 450F

Place springform on sheetpan and fill with cheesecake mixture.

Bake 20 minutes. Cake should be 1/2 inch over rim and golden brown.

Lower temp to 250 by opening door and setting temp.

Bake another 35 minutes, until internal temp is 145.

Cool 15 minutes, then run knife around edges.

Cool for 1 hour, cover and refrigerate for no less than 12 hours (overnight).

Release springform sides once cake is chilled.

Plastic wrap and refrigerate and cake will hold for 10 days.

September 2019

Chocolate Espresso Creme Brulee

Ingredients:
2 cups heavy cream
1 tbsp instant espresso powder
5 oz. bittersweet chocolate, chopped
6 egg yolks
3 tbsps sugar
1 tsp vanilla extract
1/4 cup sugar (for topping)
chocolate-covered espresso beans for garnish (optionally use seasonal fruit and whipped cream)

Instructions:

1. In a medium saucepan, bring the cream and espresso powder to a simmer. Whisk to help dissolve the espresso granules. Remove from heat and add the chocolate while the cream is still hot. Mix until smooth and set aside.
2. In a large bowl, whisk the egg yolks, sugar, and vanilla together. Slowly add the chocolate mixture to the egg mixture, whisking to combine. Strain through a sieve. Ladle the custard into containers and place containers in a water bath, half way up containers.
3. Bake at 325 for approximately 10 minutes, carefully checking whether it has set or not. A slight looseness in the middle is what you are looking for. Remove from oven and let cool in water bath.

Gayle's Lemon Tart

Teresa's sister, Gayle, raves about our lemon tart, so I named this after her for her love and enthusiasm. I try to take it when we trek to Ashdown AK to visit her and Joe.

Brown Butter Tart Shells

6 tbsp. unsalted butter, cubed

1 tbsp. canola oil

⅛ tsp. kosher salt

3 tbsp. water

1 tbsp. sugar

1 cup flour

1. Make the crust: Heat oven to 400°. Stir butter, water, oil, sugar, and salt in a heatproof bowl; bake until butter is bubbling and lightly brown at edges, about 20 minutes.
2. Remove from oven and stir in flour until dough comes together. Press dough into bottom and up sides of five 4″ tart pans (or one large 9″ tart). Using a fork, prick dough all over.
3. Bake until cooked through, 10–12 minutes; let cool.

Lemon Curd

12 tbs butter

3 large eggs

1 cup sugar

1 cup lemon juice

3/8 cup sour cream

4 egg yolks

1 tbs cornstarch

6 tsp lemon zest

1. Use the double boiler method to heat the butter and sour cream, about 2 minutes.
2. In a separate bowl whisk or blend the eggs, yolk, sugar and cornstarch until fully incorporated. Add the lemon and zest to the egg mixture.
3. Add the lemon and egg mixture to the butter and sour cream and cook, stirring constantly for 3 minutes until set. You will see and feel the curd come together and you can decide on the thickness you want by taking the curd off the heat. It will set thicker as it cools. Chill completely.
4. Fill the tart shell with lemon curd and hold refrigerated or serve.

Dedication

Thanks to all of our family and to our crews that supported us over the years.   You crew members know who you are, Leo, Maria, Eddy, Heather, Hannah, Mike, Ryan, Sarah, Shelly, Jordan, Nick and Samantha. Critically important was our loyal guests, many who visited us every week while we were open. Thanks Tom & Linda, Hul & Nancy, Holly, Doug and Debi, Kevin & Rene, Zoe & Joe, Keith & Kathleen, Kyle & De Ann, Randy & Susan, Candace, Mike & Sarah, Dawn & Paul and those we are forgetting.

Kimber is our official mascot for Sip & Savor. She was with me, sitting on the front porch while planning the restaurant. She was with us through all the long days and nights, sometimes in the yard chasing rabbits, sometimes just napping. She was occasionally with us inside, but don't tell the health department!! And Kimber was with us through the decision to close, and for our move to Granbury. Kimber passed in August 2023 at 14 years of age. A perfect companion that we will always remember, and love.

www.ingramcontent.com/pod-product-compliance
Lightning Source LLC
Chambersburg PA
CBHW042051100726
47973CB00014B/217